10 KEYS TO REVENUE GROWTH

IT'S NOT HARD, IT'S BUSINESS

Fundamental steps to help business owners
learn what it takes to grow their business
and increase revenue

D1601612

GARY FURR

It's Not Hard, It's Business
by Gary Furr
Published by Gary Furr, LLC, Portland, Oregon
garyfurrconsulting.com

ISBN 978-1-7311-9423-7

IT'S NOT HARD, IT'S BUSINESS

Table of Contents

CHAPTER ONE

Business Doesn't Have to Be So Hard

Business is really very simple if you know what to do, yet I have found that most business owners make it far more difficult than it needs to be. In their desire to make their business a success, I have seen business owners work harder and harder doing the same things they have always done, expecting different results. That does not work.

Statistics paint a grim picture of the chances to succeed in business. Only 5 percent of all businesses ever do more than a million dollars in gross revenue per year. Only .004 percent of businesses do more than $5 million in gross revenue per year, and even less do more than $10 million in revenue. The life span of a business is even more dismal. After one year, 50 percent of all businesses fail. By the fifth year, another 80 percent of those businesses have failed; and by year ten, 96 percent of all small businesses have gone out of business—and that does not mean that the 4 percent that are left are making money.

The message to business owners is clear: You cannot leave your business success to chance or luck. Furthermore, what got you to your current point most likely will not get you where you want to go.

To beat the odds, you have to take control of your business and learn the necessary skills to grow and sustain your business. You did not go into business to just get by, but if you are not proactive about ensuring your success, then just getting by or failure will be the end result.

If you really want to take your business to a new level and ensure your competitive advantage, profitability, and success, you need to learn and master the steps to sustainable business growth and acceleration. The process of achieving success means you can never stop learning and you must continually upgrade your skill sets and capabilities.

The secret in business is mastering the little things that can make significant differences in your business. It is the little things done consistently over time that add up to great success. If you want to grow your business, it starts with you.

This is about understanding some of the foundational steps necessary to building a strong business that can achieve what you have always dreamed. Every building has a foundation, and if the foundation is not strong, the building will fall. Fortunately, you can shore up the foundation of your business with the steps in this book. Here is your quick and dirty guide to business success.

CHAPTER TWO

Accelerate Your Business Growth

Simple steps make all the difference in business growth. I discovered these steps in the process of interacting with hundreds of business owners; more importantly, I have used these principles to help my clients achieve from 30 percent to over 400 percent increases in their bottom-line results.

This short book cannot possibly cover all the aspects of business success, but the following fundamental steps have power to accelerate growth and increase your odds of success:

1. Mindset
2. Strategy
3. Clear direction
4. A map and plan of action
5. Focus
6. Discipline
7. Knowing your numbers
8. Understanding your cash flow
9. Knowing your banker
10. Paying your taxes

Think of business growth acceleration like driving a stick shift. You have to start your car in first gear and then shift through the other gears to achieve the desired acceleration. Just like driving, you cannot start in third gear. As you shift through the gears and build momentum, the effort required of the engine is lessened. It is the same in your business. There are no shortcuts. You have to shift through the gears, and all the gears have to be working in order to build and achieve success.

I know so many business owners and executives today who are working harder and harder, running on the treadmill of life faster and faster, but they are not getting anywhere.

You do not have to work harder and harder to make your business a success. Putting your head down and doing the same things—just harder and faster—hoping that things will change is not a good strategy. So stop it! Stop thinking that if you just work harder, your business will improve. You do not have to work harder, you do need to work smarter and more efficiently. The key principles in this book can help guide you along the path to success.

CHAPTER THREE

Mindset Matters

Mindset it the foundation of all success. It is tempting to think that skills are, but that is not what I have observed throughout my years in helping to lead companies toward greater success. What I have seen is that if your mindset is not right, success will be elusive.

Like everyone, business owners often have internal stories that they are telling themselves. These stories originate in their past, yet still manage to get in the way of their success. Unfortunately, these past stories, or self-limiting beliefs, can prevent you from achieving the level of success you dream of attaining. Your limiting beliefs do not merely exist inside your own mind. They have real-world consequences, and that is why they must be addressed in order to achieve success.

During my second visit with one particular client, he went into a twenty-minute explanation as to why he had not been successful thus far and why he would not be successful moving forward. He elaborated on his past as well as his relationship with his father, and he said that he was doomed to failure. After he finished his story, I politely told him that this was complete nonsense. He looked at me with astonishment and asked why. I explained to him that it was like he was driving his car by looking in the rear-view mirror. How successful is that? I told him that he would not achieve the level of success he desired when he believed it would never happen. He was allowing his past and the mindset that had developed there to control his future. Of course we cannot change the past, but we can learn from it. In the big picture, it does not really matter where you came from, it only matters where you are and where you want to go. I love what Tony Robbins, author and success coach, says about the past: "What if your past happened for you, and not to you?"[1]

You have the freedom to let go of the past and reinvent your future. You need to learn how to thrive, not survive. If you want your business to get better, then you have to get better. If you want things to change, then you have got to change. As Dean Graziosi says in his book *Millionaire Success Habits*, "We want to be the thermostat not the thermometer."[2]

How to Feed Your Mind

Our minds are not unlike our bodies: We are what we eat. If we feed our minds with negativity, we will get negativity. If we feed our minds with positive information, we will get positivity in return. Whatever we allow in is what occupies our thoughts. Our minds do not discriminate between destructive input and constructive input. Both have an effect on our physical reality.

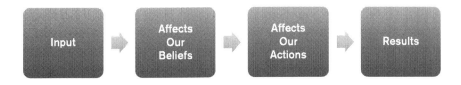

If you continually tell yourself negative thoughts, you will start to believe those thoughts and they will have a direct effect on your actions, which will eventually get you exactly what you were thinking. The opposite is also true, of course. If you feed your mind with good thoughts and positive input, you will get positive results. Success will come to you if you are determined to be successful and you intentionally adopt a positive mindset. Because you have the power within you to change what you believe is possible, you can affect what actually becomes possible.

I personally have gone on a no-news diet. The news on TV, no matter what channel you listen to, has more negative news than positive. Steven Pinker, a Canadian-American cognitive psychologist, wrote an article for *The Guardian* magazine entitled "The Media Exaggerates Negative News. This Distortion has Consequences." In the article he says that every day the news is filled with stories about war, terrorism, crime, pollution and a host of other negative topics. He states that even magazine covers are covered with negative topics and crises of some sort or another.

Pinker says, "Whether or not the world really is getting worse, the nature of news will interact with the nature of cognition to make us think it is. News is about things that happen, not things that don't happen."[3] He went on to say that the news can and likely will distort our view of the world, and the consequences of negative news are negative.

Reprogram Your Negative Thinking

I often tell clients if they have negative thought patterns that have been ingrained over time, they should think of the antithesis or exact opposite of that thought and start developing a mantra of saying the positive over and over until they change their belief system. A good way to do this is to write down the positive opposite of your negative belief and read it out loud every day, morning and night, in order to reprogram your subconscious mind. This sounds rather simplistic, but it actually works and gets your subconscious mind engaged in helping to change your belief system.

Fix in your mind what you want to achieve and write it down. Any idea that you write down and repeat verbally day after day will indeed program your subconscious mind to ensure you are moving in the right direction. Your state of mind often determines the story you come up with. You need a story that empowers you, not one that disempowers you.

In his book *Think and Grow Rich*, Napoleon Hill says, "The power of auto-suggestion is the agency of central thought through which an individual may voluntarily feed his sub-conscious mind on thoughts of creative nature, or by neglect permit thoughts of a destructive nature."[4]

Success comes to those who are determined to be successful and adopt a positive mindset with a definite purpose. We all have the power to make the little choices in our lives that can alter our lives forever. If you do not believe that, I recommend Viktor Frankl's book, *Man's Search for Meaning*. Viktor was a prisoner of war in a Nazi concentration camp. He saw his family murdered, and he endured bizarre experiments on his body. He came to the conclusion that while he did not have physical freedom, he did have the freedom to choose his response to what was happening to him. It is not so much what happens to us that has the greatest impact on us and those around us, but our response to what happens.

You should make a concerted effort to spend time around people who are playing at a higher level than you. I have heard it said that we become the sum total of the five people we spend the most time with. Most people hang around with people playing at a lower level. Do not be the smartest person in the room. Invest in yourself and get around people that are smarter and more successful than you. Ask questions and learn. The best investment you can make is in yourself.

The foundation of success is mindset. By mastering the little things that impact your mindset, you can make an enormous difference in your business, and in your life.

Success Steps

1. Stand guard at the door of your mind.
2. Be careful and intentional about what you allow into your mind.
3. Pay attention to any negative self-talk that you have become accustomed to saying without thinking about it.
4. Counter any negative self-talk with a positive mantra that you repeat twice a day.
5. Focus on the positive, not the negative.
6. Write down some positive supporting statements, and repeat them daily.
7. Find a way to feed and strengthen your mind every single day.
8. Ask yourself this question on a somewhat regular basis: What are the things I am going to do to improve my mindset?

CHAPTER FOUR

Strategy Counts

Strategy is a bigger topic than this short book can cover. I mention it here, however, because strategy is one of the fundamental steps of success. We will talk about it briefly, with the understanding that strategy is a topic worthy of its own book. In fact, two of the best books on strategy I have read are *Good Strategy/Bad Strategy*, by Richard Rumelt, and *Strategy and the Fat Smoker*, by David Maister. There is a lot of confusion as to what strategy really is, but what strategy is not is vision and goal setting (topics I will cover later).

It Starts with a Need

In graduate school one of the instructors (a business person, not a professor) told us something that I have never forgotten. He said that business was relatively simple and amounts to this: Find a need, fill the need, and collect a check. Then he added, don't screw it up in the middle because most businesses owners do screw it up.

To me this is the heart of good strategy: finding the need and fig-uring out how you will meet that need. Knowing what problem you are solving and how you will solve it is strategy. Then you organize your business in such a way that it can meet the needs in the most efficient and effective manner.

According to research by Nathan Furr and Jeff Dyer in their book *The Innovators Method*, the most successful companies do not just offer products that are easier to use, they offer products that delight their customers. How do you delight your customers? By meeting their needs and solving their problems. The authors go on to say that you have to first deeply understand the customer's problem, pain, or desire. They describe it as the job to be done and it comes from un-derstanding a problem in a way that others have not, and then going beyond the customer's expectations in providing a solution.

As Richard Rumelt says in *Good Strategy/Bad Strategy*, a good strategy has an essential logical structure and a set of coherent ac-tions. He illustrates with Apple and Steve Jobs: "In 1997 two months from bankruptcy, Steve Jobs returned to Apple as interim CEO. Steve did the unexpected and shrunk Apple down to a more suitable size to be a niche producer in the highly competitive personal computer business."[5]. He cut Apple back in order for the business to survive. Steve's strategy was to go after and address the fundamental problem of survival with a focused and coordinated set of actions. Where is Apple today?

In essence, strategy is an intentional focus and alignment of re-sources that delivers maximum and measurable results to meet the customers' needs.

Success Steps

1. What problem are you going to solve?
2. Where is the problem located?
3. How will you solve it?
4. How will you organize your company in order to solve the problem?
5. How will you add value to your customers?

!

CHAPTER FIVE

Choose
Your
Direction

Many times, when business owners are struggling, they think they just need to work harder and harder and that will change things. It rarely does. What *does* work is slowing down and taking a bird's-eye view of your business to observe the current state or your reality. Where is your business today? Be honest with yourself. You have to know where you really are. There cannot be any self-deception or unwillingness to see reality; just tell the truth.

I know slowing down does not sound like the key to success. In fact, it probably sounds like the last thing you should do. But trust me: Running faster and faster in the wrong direction is a critical mistake. Stop and observe where you are. Does it look anything like what you envisioned it would look like when you started your business? Are you where you thought you would be both personally and professionally?

One of my early clients, we will call him Tim, had been working in his business for five years and had finally made a small profit. He was discouraged that the hard work and effort had not paid off as he originally thought it should, so he called me. He explained what was going on in his business and that he had decided to sell it and do something else. Together we came to the conclusion that he would sell his business in two years. In order to do so there were some things we needed to accomplish in order to make the business more appealing to a potential buyer. The first step was to completely understand his current state. The next step was to determine a clear direction. Since we knew he would sell the business in two years, we worked backwards from there. In doing so, we determined that he would need to start documenting his processes and procedures so that anyone new could come in and figure out how to run the business without Tim's involvement.

The next step was to develop a plan of action on how to bridge the gap between his current state and his desired future to sell the business. Then, of course, he would have to begin executing on the plan. This is where the difficulty came in for Tim. He had not been focused on his business. He was distracted by a variety of things, including social media, so much so that he would come to work every day but accomplish very little.

With clear direction and a map for the business, we made a plan of action to get Tim to be more focused on his business. I had Tim promise me that he would give me four hours a day, from 8 a.m. until noon, of complete focus on his business. He was responsible for eliminating any distractions that took him away from that focus. After noon, I told him, I did not care what he did. He could go play golf, dive into social media, play video games, anything. It did not matter as long as he gave me those four hours of uninterrupted time every day, and he agreed. Once Tim had a clear direction and a plan of action, he became motivated to be intensely focused on his business to get it ready to sell.

A funny thing happened along the journey. The very next year Tim's business had a 540 percent increase in revenue. Suddenly Tim was highly motivated by the results he was getting and began second-guessing his decision to sell his business. He had a clear vision of where he wanted to go, a map to his destination, and a plan of action on how to get his business there. He had also been intensely focused for at least four hours per day over many months, which generated amazing results. Now he was highly motivated and no longer wanted to sell the business. It is remarkable what a clear sense of direction can do.

Working Backwards

Before you begin any journey, you need to know where you are setting out from, your starting point. I recommend developing a personal and business balance sheet to determine where you are currently. There are numerous items you can address on your balance sheet. Here are some questions you can ask yourself:

- What is my current financial situation?
- How many hours per week am I working?
- Am I in control of my business or is the business running me?
- How much time am I spending working *in* the business versus *on* the business?
- If I take an extended vacation, will the business continue to operate smoothly?
- Am I able to regularly spend time with family and friends?
- Do I have time for volunteer work or other interests outside of work?

Of course you should add your own questions based on matters important to you and your quality of life. Once you have been completely honest about where you are, it is time to think about what you want the future to look like for your business and your personal life.

I stress this with all of my clients: Do not neglect to consider your personal life. You need to acknowledge what you want both personally and in your business. You have a life, and more often than not your personal and business lives are intimately intertwined. You cannot consider one without considering the other.

I advise creating a vision of the future five years from this day. You want to go out five years from now and describe what that is going to look like for you in your business and your personal life. How many employees do you want to have? How much money do you want to make? How big of a business do you want? How many weeks of vacation do you want to take? Describe it in writing, but stick to about six or seven items. Then work backwards from that.

If you want to be at this particular future state in five years, where do you need to be three years from now? Write that down as well. Use the same six or seven items, and describe what each looks like in three years. Then work backwards again: Where do you want to be a year from now? If you need to be at a certain point in three years, where do you need to be a year from now?

What would your business look like if money, time, and energy were no object?

You need to be bold when you think about this and describe it. Write it down, and read it often. Give yourself permission to dream big. It is your life and your business. Why not dream big?

Do not let your small business make you small-minded. This is a common pitfall. You did not start your business by thinking small. Why not think really big and imagine the future that you want? John F. Kennedy was not thinking small when he announced we would put a man on the moon in ten years. We did not even have the technology to do it then. It had to be created. Think outside of your own box. And if you are unable to think outside the box because you are in the box, get a mentor or a coach to help you to see more clearly.

Put It in Writing

Writing it all down is part of the process. It is not sufficient to see it in your mind, you must write it down. Maybe that seems tedious, or even childish, but do not talk yourself out of doing it. Your mind is a powerful tool if you put it to work on your behalf. The shear act of writing down your vision of the future puts your subconscious mind to work to help you to make it happen, even when you are not thinking about it.

I remember hearing author and motivational speaker Brian Tracy tell a crowd that if they took a blank piece of paper and wrote down ten things they wanted to accomplish in the next year and then folded the piece of paper in half, dated it, put it away, and did not look at it for the entire year, a year later they would have accomplished seven or eight of the items on the list. He guaranteed it. This is due to putting the power of the subconscious mind to work.

Now imagine how powerful this principle would be if you not only wrote it down, but you read it every day, even twice a day. You can dream and create the future you want by putting the power of your subconscious mind to work to help you achieve your dreams.

Think about it this way: If you decide to take a thousand-mile journey, you need to know where you want to end up. Certainly when you board an airplane, you know where you are going. If you do not pay attention to where you want to end up, you most likely will not arrive at your destination. It is no different in life or in business.

When I worked in the corporate world, I had an airplane at my disposal to save time getting from one location to another. Traveling at 160 mph in an airplane gets you where you want to go in a big hurry, but you had better know where that is.

Don't Be Like Alice

In the story of *Alice in Wonderland*, Alice is looking for a way out of Wonderland. When she comes to a crossroad, she turns to the Cheshire Cat sitting there and says, "I just wanted to ask you which way I ought to go?" The Cheshire Cat then tells her that it depends on where she wants to be. Alice says she does not know, and the Cheshire Cat smiles and says, "Then it does not matter which way you go."

Without a clear direction, you will be just like Alice. It does not matter which road you take if you do not know where you want to go—but of course it is unlikely you will end up where you want to be. Surprisingly, few business owners take the time to set a destination for their business (or for their personal life). How can you define success if you do not know exactly what you want the future to look like?

Not only do you need to know where you want to go, you have to know where you are currently if you are going to get from A to B. A is your current state, and B is your destination or desired future. To chart a course, you must be truthful about where you are. No pretending. No denial. If you took a 30,000-foot view of your business and your personal life, how would you describe it? That is your current state. Understanding that is a critical part of charting a course to the future.

I suggest to my clients that they read their five-year, three-year, and one-year visions every day. Doing so is a powerful tool for creating the future you want and putting your subconscious mind to work for you.

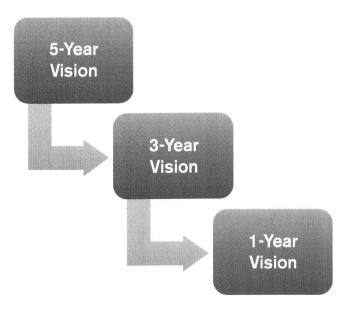

Success Steps

1. Spend time understanding your current state or reality.
2. Envision your business and personal life five years from now.
3. Work backwards to plan what you want your business and life to look like three years from now and one year from now to keep you on track toward your five-year vision.
4. Write this vision out.
5. Read it every day to put the power of your subconscious mind to work.

CHAPTER SIX

Map
Your
Course

I was doing some volunteer work for a nonprofit, and I learned that three years earlier, they had had a consultant come in and develop a strategy and vision of the future for the organization. Unfortunately, the vision had not been accomplished, so the organization went back to the drawing board with a new consultant. They developed a grand strategic plan for the future, and everyone was excited—until the consultant left. At that point everyone wondered how they would achieve this grand strategic plan. Vision and strategies are useless without a map or plan of action to get you where you want to go. Strategies need to be executed or they will not serve the organization.

It is not uncommon for organizations to fail to enact their vision. But more common, in my experience, is that business owners and CEOs are so busy being busy running day-to-day operations that they do not have the time to stop and analyze their current state and determine their desired future. If they do, they do not take the time to chart a detailed course between those two points.

Check Your Coordinates

A map is there to guide you from where you are to where you want to go. Furthermore, a map helps you to see the most efficient route to take. Of course a map is only valuable if you know where you are currently, hence the need to be brutally honest about where you are starting from. The business environment is constantly changing and you will need to refer to your map and make slight adjustments along the way. If you develop a map but then do not refer to it often, it is not going to help you achieve the results you want in the most efficient way possible.

As I previously mentioned, I used to fly an airplane to save time going between locations. I could set the airport coordinates or airport identifier for where I wanted to go along with the GPS, but if I did not continually check my location and refer to the map, I could easily get off course due to crosswinds or other factors. I had to continually check the environment and location, and make adjustments. It is the same with your map of your business and where you want to go. You have to continually make sure you are on course and make the appropriate adjustments to stay there. The business environment is changing constantly like a crosswind, and you need to continually make course corrections to create a successful future.

I once heard motivational speaker Brendon Burchard ask this question: "When is the best time to have a map if you are going hiking in the woods? The answer: Before you enter the woods."[6] If you do not have a map and there are no trail markers, it is not difficult to get lost in the woods. Sometimes navigating business can be like finding your way in a forest. Why make it harder on yourself than it needs to be? Your map will be the guidepost on your journey toward your desired future.

I have climbed Mount St. Helens five times. On my first climb I was told that hikers had to be very careful when descending the mountain due to how the ground sloped off to the east. People tended to follow the natural contour of the land without realizing it and would eventually get off course and get lost. The U.S. Forest Service eventually solved this problem by installing large wood poles embedded in a pile of rocks to mark the path to prevent hikers from getting lost. They essentially created a visual map to follow to keep people on track.

Mark Your Own Path

You can mark your own path toward your future. I recommend using ninety-day increments. What are you going to do in the next ninety days that will move you closer to your one-year vision? Goal-setting marks your path, and meeting those goals provides ongoing propulsion to power you toward your desired destination.

Write your ninety-day goals down, and read them every day.

Setting goals is a common practice of high achievers. According to Brendon Burchard's research for his book *High Performance Habits*, "High performers have a deliberate approach in planning their days, projects, and tasks compared to underperformers." He adds that "the fundamentals of becoming more productive are setting goals and maintaining energy and focus. No goals, no focus. Productivity starts with goals."[7]

One of the great benefits of these ninety-day goals is that they prevent you from getting off course. Whenever you have a difficult decision to make, ask yourself just one question: Does this take us closer to our one-year vision of the future or further away? With the ninety-day goals marking your trail, the decision should then be easy.

By repeating your clear ninety-day goals daily, you will empower yourself and your organization to pursue those goals, rather than getting ensnared in the day-to-day clutter or non-essential activities. You will also be building your belief in what is possible. Your beliefs affect your actions, which has a direct effect on your results.

Your success cannot be left to chance or good fortune. You have to do the hard work. Part of that hard work is going through this envisioning and goal-setting process. In doing so, you are laying the foundation for success.

I love the statement from Brendon Burchard, who said, "When you knock on the door of opportunity, don't be surprised to see hard work standing there, when you open the door."[8] No one said that business would be easy, but it does not have to be so complicated. Chunk it down into manageable pieces.

Success Steps

1. Spend some time thinking about the ninety-day goals that will help you get to your one-year vision of the future.
2. Write them down.
3. Believe in yourself and trust that your dreams are possible.
4. Read your ninety-day goals every day.

CHAPTER SEVEN

Focus Means Power

Once you have a clear direction for your business and your personal life coupled with a plan of action to achieve the success you desire, you need to develop an intense focus on that plan of action. People often fail to consider the power of intense focus. Water at 60,000 pounds PSI can cut through two inches of steel, but that same water when unfocused will just splash on the steel and create rust. Intense focus is a necessary requirement for success.

Tim, the client I mentioned who was so distracted by social media as well as email and phone calls from his friends and family, was not aware of all the time he spent interacting with others. The reality is that he was distracted by other people's agendas rather than being focused on his own. Even though he spent most of his day at the office, he was unproductive and accomplished little. Another client I interact with is also very distracted by social media. He leads an active social life and spends a great deal of his time reacting to incoming text messages, email, and other notifications that light up his cell phone. Perhaps not surprisingly, his employees have followed suit and they too are spending a great deal of time on social media and little on being productive.

The High Cost of Distraction

Every day in your business you are burning through cash—and you do not even know where it is going! I can hear you now: I bet you think you are the exception. You know I have not looked at your numbers, so how dare I predict such waste? I dare because I have observed that constant distractions are impeding productivity—yours, your staff's, and your employees'. This is costing your business some serious money.

A recent study found that the time wasted as a result of constant distractions is costing the U.S. economy $997 billion every year, and 89 percent of employees do not complete their top three tasks each day due to distractions. Employees are wasting 759 hours each year due to workplace distractions. That equals 19 weeks—almost five months every year! One study found that on average, workers check their email forty times a day, even when there has been no notification or email alert.[9] These distractions are like kryptonite. They are killing your productivity, which has a direct effect on your profitability.

Studies show that every time we get distracted, it takes approximately 23 minutes to get refocused. To make matters worse, the average U.S. worker feels the pull of distraction every three minutes.

You can change this negative pattern if you are willing to take charge of your time. Perhaps it is not time management that is your biggest issue these days, but self-management.

Most people that I run into underestimate the need to develop an unapologetic focus on their plan of action. You need to eliminate the distractions in your life that prevent you from achieving your success and take genuine action on your goals.

Determine Your High-Value Activities

What is the highest and best use of your time, energy, and money? I recommend really considering the question and writing your answers down. Now, remember that time, energy, and money are all limited resources. You only have so much energy, and each night, when the clock hits midnight, you are out of time. How can you focus on applying these assets to achieve the maximum results?

Many have heard of the 80/20 rule, which originated with the Italian economist Vilfredo Pareto during the nineteenth century. He wrote a mathematical model for income distribution in Italy and found that 80 percent of the land was owned by 20 percent of the people. It turns out that the Pareto principle applies to just about everything in nature. The 80/20 rule demonstrates that a minority of inputs or effort, 20 percent, usually leads to 80 percent of the results. Pareto even found this to be true with his garden peas: 20 percent of his plants generated 80 percent of the harvest.[10]

As you can see, the 20 percent is critical. What is the 20 percent of your time, energy, and money that will generate 80 percent of your results? You need to get intensely focused on this 20 percent—it is one of the keys to your success.

By thinking about this 20 percent, you will begin to think more strategically about your business and elevate your focus, thinking, and actions to a higher level. Business as usual will not do it. Business as usual will not get you the kind of success you desire. You have to get focused on the important high-value activities, the 20 percent that delivers the greatest return of your investment of time, energy, and money. Determine what those activities are.

Without focus, people tend to become consumed with non-essential, low-priority activities, which causes them to get overwhelmed and then waste their time, talent, energy, and money on the wrong type of work. Determine what your 80 percent activities are. Write them down and stop doing them by eliminating them, automating them, handing them off, or outsourcing them. The idea is to create a Stop Doing list to remind you to stop wasting your time on low-value activities that are not the highest and best use of your time.

It is easy to get busy being busy and lose sight of what is most important. Then life becomes complex, cloudy, confusing, and stressful. You can combat that tendency by knowing your 20 percent and focusing your time and energy there.

Success Steps

1. Eliminate distractions. Know what gets in your way. Do you need to turn off your phone? Silence your notifications? Delete social media from your phone?
2. Find the 20 percent in your life, and write those things down.
3. Read them every day, and focus on that 20 percent.
4. Find your 80 percent activities and take steps to eliminate or hand off those low-value tasks.
5. Create a Stop Doing list.

CHAPTER EIGHT

Discipline Delivers

The word *discipline* gets a bad rap. Sure, it can mean punishment, but I think that meaning taints our understanding of the discipline that we need to employ to produce the outcomes we are looking for. Discipline is required to remain focused and to stay hard at work every day and to persevere. As Martin Seligman, the author of *Learner Optimism*, says, "Success has more to do with resilience and persistence than skill set."[11]

World-class athletes, famous musicians, and elite military teams such as the Navy Seals all have the same thing in common: They express their talents with predictable precision, which is achieved through disciplined and repeated practice. They are in the habit of practicing over and over until they get it right.

I love to watch the Oregon Ducks play football. When Chip Kelly was their head coach, he had his players disciplined into a fine-tuned machine that executed flawlessly almost every play. This was developed through repeated practice, discipline, being intensely focused, and great communication. The players were so disciplined at their craft that they could run play after play without going into a huddle, causing the opposing defense to become exhausted.

In *Good to Great*, author Jim Collins asserts that great companies have a strong culture of discipline. If discipline leads to greatness, then the lack of discipline leads to chaos, confusion, and unpredictable results. Successful people have the discipline to stay at it and work to continually improve on what they are doing.

Stop Dabbling

As a business owner, if you are going to dabble in your business, you are probably not going to achieve the level of success you desire. Dabblers rarely succeed at what they are doing. Full commitment and discipline are required.

What skill set is preventing you from taking your business to the next level? There is an old saying that knowledge is power, however, I no longer believe this to be true. Everyone now has access to all the knowledge they could ever want and probably more than they need. You can learn any skill that you are lacking from the comfort of your own office or home, and you can hire a mentor or coach to help you take your business to a whole new level.

There is no reason a lack of knowledge should be holding you back, but lack of discipline may be. Do not think about perfection. The goal is to develop the discipline to keep at your goals every day and make improvements. It is about making progress. Take some action today.

I believe the way to stay disciplined is to block off time on your calendar to be intensely focused. Working in chunks of time without distractions has the power to generate tremendous results. Use your calendar to block off chunks of time, and do not allow anything to violate it. It may be a difficult habit to start, but once you start to see progress, it will motivate you to stay at it.

Look at your calendar. What does it look like? Do you have blocks of time to be focused on your priorities for the day or for the week? If not, it is unlikely that you will accomplish them.

Keep the pressure on to stick with it. Back when I used to fly, it would often be necessary to make a course correction. In this instance, I would turn the yoke on the airplane to go toward a new direction, but if I did not keep the pressure on the yoke, the airplane would spin back to the direction it had been going due to momentum. Work is no different. If you do not keep the pressure on, you will revert to your previous habits. Keep the pressure on your own yoke to maintain your direction and momentum.

Success Steps

1. Use your calendar to block off time each day for your top three priorities.
2. Tackle your list in order. Do not move on to the next item before completing the one before it.
3. Block off time to return phone calls, emails, and texts.
4. Stick to it day after day and watch how much you get accomplished.

CHAPTER NINE

Manage the Numbers

The numbers drive everything in your business. Without a complete understanding of your numbers, you really do not know how your business is doing. You cannot manage your business from your checkbook.

When I watch football, how do I know who is winning and who is losing while I watch the game? I look at the scoreboard to know the actual score, the time remaining, the down, and how many yards to the next first down. Even the referees, the coaches, and the quarterback pay attention to the scoreboard. Reading the scoreboard is the only real way to know which team is winning and which is losing.

Use Your Scoreboards Wisely

It is the same in your business. The primary scoreboards in your business are the P&L (profit and loss), the balance sheet, and the cash flow projection. How else do you know if you are winning or losing? Income statements (also known as the P&L) are great for comparison to measure progress in the business. For example, you can use it to compare the current quarter with the previous quarter, or the current quarter to the same quarter the previous year. The P&L is like a movie—it covers a period of time, such as the first quarter (Q1), second quarter (Q2), or year to date (YTD). The balance sheet is similar. It is a good comparison tool, and it works like a snapshot in time. It covers a particular date, like the end of the fiscal year (December 31) or the end of a quarter, and looks at the information on that particular date in time. If you are not using the P&L and balance sheet as comparison tools, you are not tracking the performance of your business.

The problem is that both the P&L and balance sheet are lagging indicators. They look backwards, and what has happened has already happened and cannot be changed. The only tool or scoreboard a business has that looks forward is the cash flow projection, which takes all the information from the P&L except depreciation and amortization because they do not use cash, and then adds in debt payments, which are a use of cash but do not show up on the P&L. The problem that many business owners get into is that they look at their P&L and net income and think that is cash. It is not cash but the theory of cash, because any principle payments on debt are not recorded on the P&L but are recorded on the cash flow projection.

Many business owners I run into are not paying attention to their scoreboards. They are essentially running their business by the seat of their pants, hoping they are winning the game, but they really do not know. They are playing a guessing game with their future and the future of their employees.

When I fly an airplane, I have to be able to read the instruments on the dashboard. I might be able to get by on a clear, sunny day, but what happens if a storm comes in, or I get caught in fog? In those circumstances, if I am unable to read the instruments, I am probably going to die. It is your responsibility to know how to read the critical instruments in your business: the P&L, the balance sheet, and the cash flow projection.

Learn the Language of Business

If you are an entrepreneur with a particular skill set and that skill is not accounting, then I would suggest you take some online or on-site courses to sharpen your skills. You do not need to become an accountant, you do need a basic understanding of accounting. I also recommend *Finance for the Non-Financial Manager* by Gene Siciliano. Ignorance is not bliss when the success of your business is at stake.

I have a favorite restaurant in Portland, Oregon, where I like to eat. The food is always amazing and the menu changes regularly based on what is fresh at the time. I love to sit at the chef's counter and watch the cooks work their magic. If you consider the consistent and flawless food they produce, you realize that the chefs have mastered the language of cooking—teaspoons, tablespoons, cups, pinches, temperature, seasoning, and much more—allowing them to produce amazing results. The language is such a part of them, it is as if they have become native speakers.

It is the same with musicians. The ones that move us with their songs have learned the language of music—flats, sharps, chords, and keys. Their investment in learning the language produces the compositions we spend our time listening to and enjoying.

When flying, it was critical that I learn all the aspects of flying, such as the pre-flight check list, taking off, actually flying, and landing (which was always the most challenging aspect). I had to learn the language of flying in order to make good decisions. I had to understand what levers to push or pull and to what degree. If I had been lazy and had not taken the time to learn this language, it would have been disastrous to my life and the lives of my passengers.

As a business owner, you are responsible for learning the language of business— accounting. Understanding the P&L and balance sheet and how they are interconnected is critical to the success of your business. If you are unable to understand and speak the language, you are putting your business in jeopardy.

The problem is that the P&L and balance sheet both look backwards. The information you are receiving has already happened, and you cannot do much to change it. The past is important, but what about the future? Most of the mistakes in business are due to not knowing your real numbers. You thought you were going 75 mph, but you were really only going 30. You thought you had a full tank of gas, but you were only half full. That's why you need a cash flow projection.

Success Steps

1. Learn the language of business.
2. Review your P&L and balance sheet weekly.
3. Compare months, quarters, and YTDs to the previous year's results.
4. Consider what adjustments you can make to manage the numbers in a more profitable way.

CHAPTER TEN

Know Your Cash Flow

The cash flow projection is the only tool or scoreboard you have that looks ahead at what is coming in your business so you can forecast your cash needs. If you do not have cash flow, you do not have a business.

Business owners often think that net income on the bottom line of the P&L is cash, but it is actually only the theory of cash since the P&L does not account for debt payments (which are a use of cash). This highlights the need for a cash flow projection, which takes your debt payments into account.

It is no surprise that all businesses need cash to survive. Inadequate cash flow is like kryptonite to Superman; without cash your business will suffer and eventually die. Yet most business owners I meet are not tracking their cash flow. They look at their P&L and balance sheet, but they do not conduct a cash flow analysis of their business. Instead, they are managing from their checkbook.

Revenue − Expenses = Profit

Too often business owners look at net income or profit and think they are making money. Your profit is simply the amount that your revenue exceeds your expenses; it is not cash but the theory of cash since your P&L does not take into account debt service. The interest payments are accounted for, but not the debt payments, so it is easy to misunderstand how much cash you have by just looking at the P&L. You cannot spend the theory of cash, and profits are not cash. It does not matter how much profit you make if the amount of cash you receive is less than or equal to what you are spending. If you cut into your cash reserves long enough, you will eventually be broke.

Cash flow is the net amount of money that is flowing in and out of your business, and a cash flow analysis focuses on the timing of when cash comes in and when it goes out. The cash flow projection is the only tool or scoreboard you have to look ahead, and the future is where we want to go. By understanding your cash flow and how it can positively or negatively impact your business, you can make more informed decisions about how to run your business.

An important note about cash flow is that accounts receivable is not cash. There have been many businesses that have gone bankrupt with lots of accounts receivables on their books, but no cash to operate on. As you know, without cash, you cannot pay your bills. The only way to sustain your business is with positive cash flow. Sure, you can borrow money, and that is one form of cash, but it comes with a debt that you will owe. Or you can invest cash into the business to keep it afloat, but eventually you will run out of cash from investment and the ability to borrow more cash will be dependent on cash from operations.

The Value of Metrics

I like to take the financial information to another level and perform metrics on the line items within the financials. One of those helpful metrics is cost of goods sold (COGS), which is a calculation of all the costs involved with producing and selling your product, including materials, labor, warehouse space, and overhead to produce and manufacture the products you are selling. This has serious business implications. For example, I had a client who was complaining that while he made more money in 2017 than he did in 2016, his net income was a loss and he did not understand why. By doing some financial metrics I discovered that his cost of goods sold (COGS) for 2017 was over 12 percent higher than 2016, so right away he was over 12 percent behind last year's potential profit.

As a business owner, you should be performing a deep dive into your financials and performing a line item analysis as a percentage. For instance, what is COGS as a percentage of revenue? How does this compare to previous years? What is each line item of expense as a percentage of gross profit, and how does this compare to previous years? By doing such analysis we can start to develop trend lines of performance. By following the trend line, you can see how you are doing in comparison to previous years and months. This allows you to ask better questions in order to make better decisions, rather than waiting until the end of the year for a big year-end surprise. Here are some questions you should be able to answer:

1. What is your revenue per employee?
2. What is your revenue per square foot of space?
3. What is your expense per employee?
4. What is your expense per square foot of space?
5. What is your current ratio, quick ratio?
6. What is COGS as a percentage of revenue?
7. What is payroll as a percentage of gross profit?

In business, that which we measure gets addressed and improves. Many business owners do not have these answers about their businesses. If you do not, you are not alone, but it is time to change things.

CPAs and Bookkeepers

I was working with a food processor and noticed that all the goods they purchased to make their product were categorized as an expense rather than cost of goods sold. When I inquired as to why there was no COGS category, the business owner said he did not know. He said that is where their bookkeeper put them. I asked who their bookkeeper was and I was told it was a family member. I asked about their CPA because the CPA should have caught it as well. The owner explained that they had been with their CPA for years and he had never said anything. I let the business owner know that they needed a new bookkeeper and a new CPA because their current professionals were just filling in the blanks rather than advising them on how to manage and run their business. They needed better information, which would allow them to ask better questions and make better decisions.

The information needs to be accurate or you are in jeopardy of making faulty decisions based on inaccurate information. I have discovered that many CPAs and bookkeepers are not advising their clients. They are just filling in the blanks. Which one do you have? Accurate financial information and analysis is one of the keys to a successful enterprise.

Success Steps

1. Pay close attention to your P&L and balance sheet. Review them on no less than a weekly basis.
2. Create a rolling six-month cash flow projection.
3. Drill down deeper into the financials and develop some metrics to measure your performance.
4. Ask your CPA and bookkeeper to take an advisory role and help you understand your financials.

CHAPTER ELEVEN

Make Friends with Your Banker

I always ask my clients if they know their banker. Many do not. Others say they know their banker but rarely speak with them. That is a mistake. As a business owner, you need to know who your banker is and you need to be talking with them on a regular basis. The time to go and meet your banker is not when you are in trouble. Bankers, more so than ever these days, are interested in having a relationship with their customers, and that relationship likely requires you to take a proactive role.

When was the last time you invited your banker out to see your operation? When was the last time you asked to have coffee or lunch with your banker? Bankers are interested in such a relationship with business owners. They are not interested in clients that are only interested in shopping rates.

Sure you can probably get a better rate at a big bank, but when you go to the bank to renew your line of credit or to borrow more money, the individual you were working with is probably no longer there and you have to start from square one explaining your business to the new banker. There are plenty of small- to mid-market banks in your community to serve your needs, and often the bankers working for these firms have been there a long time, understand the community and your business, and have built a loyal local following for their services. Their good customers are less interested in a quarter or half basis point and more interested in the long-standing relationship. That is not much different than what you want with *your* good customers. You do not want to have to train a new banker every year.

Bankers are interested in your success. They want you to be successful because successful businesses reduce the risk to the bank. All bankers want the same thing, regardless of their size. They want to know that you have a solid business strategy, good management, and a clear direction as to where the business is going. They want to know that you have a plan of action and you are focused on achieving success in your business. Most importantly, they want to know that you understand the numbers, pay attention to them, and provide accurate and timely reporting of the information they are requesting. If you want your banker to love you, provide the information before they ask.

Success Steps

1. Get to know your banker.
2. Invite them to your place of business at least once a year.
3. Go to coffee or lunch with them to invest in the relationship.
4. Provide accurate and timely financial information.
5. Do not switch banks for a minimal change in interest rates.

CHAPTER TWELVE

Pay the Tax Man

I am running into more and more businesses that are operating in tax-avoidance mode. I completely understand the desire to not pay the tax man more than your fair share, but in minimizing your tax burden, you may be creating bigger problems.

A very successful business owner told me how they had been in tax-avoidance mode for years. At the end of each year they would pay out their profits to themselves and their employees in the form of bonuses to minimize the tax burden. The funny thing about this is that although the business was not paying as high a tax rate, the owners and their employees were paying the tax. When it became necessary to do a major remodel of their building, they went to their bank to discuss borrowing the money to remodel. The bank declined their request because they had minimal retained earnings in the business; quite simply, there were not sufficient retained earnings to support the debt load.

As a business owner in tax-avoidance mode, you are likely trying to spend your money at the end of the year to avoid taxes. This, however, is a short-term strategy that will likely have a long-term negative impact on your business. Unless you are spending that money on assets that will generate additional revenue moving forward, then you should reconsider.

Building Wealth Is Better than Avoiding Taxes

When you are thinking about avoiding taxes, you are not thinking about creating wealth. As a business owner, you should be more focused on maximizing after-tax revenue to build wealth rather than focusing on tax avoidance. Tax avoidance nearly always results in difficulty borrowing money from the bank or other lending source. The problem is that bankers do not lend from the P&L or income statement; they lend from the balance sheet. When the business owner presents their financials, the banker turns to the second page of their balance sheet and looks at retained earnings, or wealth (equity), in the business. That is where the trouble starts: The tax-avoidant business owner has not built any wealth, which makes the banker reluctant to lend them any money.

Bankers like to apply a simple ratio to your business—the debt-to-equity ratio—and this is how they set limits on how much you can borrow. Typically, it is a two-to-one ratio, meaning for every dollar of equity you have retained in your business, the bank will let you borrow two dollars. No equity or retained earnings, no borrowing. Quite simply, minimizing taxes reduces your borrowing power.

Selling Your Business

Another common pitfall related to tax avoidance occurs when it comes time to sell your business. Because you have been in tax avoidance, your business is not worth as much as it could be. Small businesses typically have a range of value at a 3–5 multiple of EBITDA—that is, earnings before interest, taxes, depreciation, and amortization. Mid-market companies tend to have a valuation of 5–7 times EBITDA. When business owners have been avoiding paying taxes, they have not maximized after-tax revenue, and therefore they have not built wealth (retained earnings). This impacts their business valuation. In other words, your business is not worth as much as it could be because you have been in tax avoidance rather than wealth creation. As my mentor and friend Phil Symchych likes to say, "Maximizing earnings will maximize your wealth."[12] We should be focusing on wealth creation, not tax avoidance.

Success Steps

1. Understand your financials.
2. Change your mindset from tax avoidance to maximizing after-tax revenue and building wealth in the business.
3. What is your EBITDA? Ask your CPA to help you determine this and track it.

CHAPTER THIRTEEN

Five Ways to Grow Your Business

Early in my consulting career I spoke with a business owner who loved to sell. He enjoyed going out and getting new customers to buy his product, and he was constantly on the hunt for more business. He was struggling with bringing new business in, however, due to a saturated market. What he had failed to do was take into consideration all his previous business and the good customers that he had done business with in the past. He was so intent on bringing new business in that he had neglected his current and past customers. I bet his competition loved this.

There are essentially five ways to grow your business. We will take a brief look at all five:

1. **Keep the customers you have:** Your current customer base is the best way to grow your business. After all, they already know you, like you, and trust you. They are used to doing business with you, and if you are performing well, they will be reluctant to switch. How do you keep the customers you have? By communicating with them more often. Do not wait

for your customers to contact you, which is usually when they have a problem. Be proactive and contact your customers. Think about it. If you are not contacting your customers, you can bet your competition is; and if your customers have not heard from you, what is to prevent them from switching their business to the individual who is showing interest in them? Revenue growth is a proactive activity, meaning you have to take the initiative to reach out and contact your customers and let them know you are thinking about them.

2. **Sell more to the customers you have:** Your current customers already are doing business with you and likely would do more business with you if you asked them, but business owners seldom ask if there is anything else that they can do to help their customers. Often business owners have other products or services that the customer could buy from them, but the customers have forgotten about those offerings. You have to keep reminding them of the other products and services you provide.

3. **Sell more often to the customers you have:** Business owners can often sell more frequently to their existing customer base, but if they are not contacting them and are just waiting for the phone to ring, then such sales are unlikely. This is another reason to be proactive and contact your customers.

4. **Get new customers:** New customer acquisition is one of the most expensive ways to get new customers. Think about how much time it takes to not only find, but to get a new customer to try you and to build up their business to a reasonable level. The customer acquisition cost is probably much higher than you think.

5. **Get rid of the problem customers or low-value customers:** These are the customers that continually cause you grief and take you away from interacting and building on the relationships you have with your good customers. It is probably taking more time than you think and causing you more stress than necessary. The best place for your problem customers is with your competition.

The equation is pretty simple. If you want to sell more, communicate more with your customers. If you want to sell less, communicate less with your customers.

Success Steps

1. Keep the good customers you already have.
2. Be proactive and contact your customers—current, past, and potential.
3. How can you better serve them and meet their needs?
4. How can you deliver more value to them than your competition does?
5. What other products or services do you offer that they have probably forgotten about?

CHAPTER FOURTEEN

Beyond Limits to Results

Years ago I was chief operations officer for the largest decid-uous shade tree nursery in the United States, located on four thousand acres in Oregon. We also had 85 acres in container-grown trees, or trees in plastic pots. We would plant fully-grown trees from our fields into containers and finish them for up to one year before we sold them.

If we didn't sell all of those trees at the end of one year, they would often become too large for their containers. When a tree be-comes too large for a container, the growth slows dramatically and the tree may even stop growing altogether. It does not matter how much fertilizer and water you give the tree, the growth is limited by the size of the container. Left for too long, these trees would actually start to deteriorate.

The same principle applies to your business. When you start your business, you plant a seed in a flowerpot and your business starts to grow. You continue to work hard in your business, and the business starts to get larger. The business continues to grow and as it does, it becomes more complex.

The problem is that eventually you are trying to grow this larger business within the small flowerpot you started out using. The systems and processes you used to start your business are no longer adequate to sustain its continual growth. It does not seem to matter how hard you work, the business will not grow and could very well become stunted. Left unaddressed this business will start to deteriorate and could eventually die.

To prevent your business from deteriorating or failing, you have to start thinking differently. You have to grow your systems and processes in order to grow your business. Stop flying by the seat of your pants. It is time to think more strategically about the systems and processes that you use to run your business on a daily basis. You cannot grow a large tree in a small flowerpot. Develop systems and processes that allow your business to continue to flourish.

If you are not getting the results you want in your business, you need to look internally. Your business is YOUR business. If it is not doing well, the responsibility is yours. To change your results, *you* need to change. For your business and personal life to be better, then you need to get better.

Do you need help getting out of your comfort zone to take your business to the next level? Be courageous and ask for help. What are you waiting for? You often cannot think outside the box when you are stuck inside the box. You need to get outside help.

It might seem far-fetched, but you can set yourself on a course to make a 1000 percent improvement in your business and personal life. Such success will not just fall into your lap. It does not take luck; it takes a dream, responsibility, and consistent effort. If you make a 1/10th of a 1 percent improvement in your business and your personal life every day, that adds up to a 0.5 percent improvement each week, which equals a 2 percent improvement each month. That is a 24 percent improvement over the course of a year, and that is a lot. If you look at it like compound interest, then that improvement (if you keep at it) would double every 2.7 years. This means in ten years you would have 1000 percent improvement in your business and your personal life.

Think about it this way: Gaining 0.5 percent a week, 2 percent each month, and 24 percent a year in improvement will get you highly motivated. It is like going to the gym and seeing that you are losing weight and looking better after putting in the effort. Why do you think there are so many mirrors in the gym? They are there so you can see your progress. This motivates you to keep going, to work out harder and more often. Results generate motivation to keep going. If you put these principles to work in your business, the results will generate the motivation to keep up the hard work.

Accountability

In order to achieve the level of success you desire in your organization, you often need someone who will hold you accountable to a higher standard, someone who is not emotionally involved in the business and who sees it from the outside looking in. You cannot read the label on the water bottle from inside the bottle. Sometimes you need someone from the outside looking in to be able to see and understand clearly what is going on. Though we wish we could, we often cannot hold ourselves accountable properly or provide the necessary insight. We need a coach, mentor, or consultant with outside experience.

It is similar to joining a gym. It helps to be held accountable by a trainer, someone who expects you to show up. Of course that same trainer also provides you with one-on-one coaching and support. The presence of a trainer demanding accountability increases your dedication to performance, and therefore increases your success. It is not any different in business. If you want to improve your results and create greater success, find a coach, mentor, or consultant who will hold you accountable.

Success Steps

1. What legacy systems and processes are you using that are holding you back? Take steps to identify them and eliminate them.
2. Consider how you can make a 1/10th of a 1 percent improvement in your business and personal life each day. Write down your plan.
3. Commit to implementing your improvement plan daily. Incorporate improvement as a habit into your day.
4. Keep the pressure on. Work hard, expecting good results.
5. If you need help, get help!

Why would you not want 1000 percent improvement—including in your bank account? These are serious results, and you can get started on achieving them today. If you need help, I am a phone call or email away: **503-312-3145 / garyfurr@garyfurrconsulting.com.**

Endnotes

1. Tony Robbins, Business Mastery Conference, London, 2016.

2. Dean Graziosi, *Millionaire Success Habits* (Dean Graziosi, 2016), 17.

3. Steven Pinker, "The Media Exaggerates Negative News. This Distortion has Consequences," *The Guardian* (theguardian. com), February 17, 2018.

4. Napoleon Hill, *Think and Grow Rich* (Shippensburg, PA: Sound Wisdom, 2016), 96.

5. Richard Rumelt, *Good Strategy/Bad Strategy* (New York: Currency, 2011), 12–13.

6. Brendon Burchard, High Performance Academy, San Jose, CA, 2017.

7. Brendon Burchard, *High Performance Habits* (Carlsbad, CA: Hay House, 2017), 175.

8. Brendon Burchard, *High Performance Habits,* 23.

9. Hardy, Darren. Insane Productivity: Gain the Ultimate Success Advantage. https://dh.darrenhardy.com/insane-productivity.

10. Crossing the Midline, "Pareto Principle and Pea Pod Pondering," www.crossingthemidline.wordpress.com, March 7, 2017.

11. Martin Seligman, Million Dollar Consulting Convention, Atlanta, GA, 2017.

12. Phil Symchych and Alan Weiss, *The Business Wealth Builders* (New York: Business Expert Press, 2015), 3.

Bibliography

Burchard, Brendon. *High Performance Habits: How Extraordinary People Become That Way*. Carlsbad, CA: Hay House, 2017.

Cunningham, Keith. *The Road Less Stupid*. Keys to the Vault Publishing, 2017.

Cunningham, Keith. *The Ultimate Blueprint for an Insanely Successful Business*, 2nd ed. Keys to the Vault Publishing, 2017.

Furr, Nathan and Paul Ahlstrom. *Nail It Then Scale It: The Entrepreneur's Guide to Creating and Managing Breakthrough Innovation*. NISI Institute, 2011.

Furr, Nathan and Jeff Dyer. *The Innovators Method: Bringing the Lean Start-up into Your Organization*. Boston: Harvard Business Review Press, 2014.

Goldfayn, Alex. *Selling Boldly: Applying the New Science of Positive Psychology to Dramatically Increase Your Confidence, Happiness, and Sales*. Hoboken, NJ: Wiley, 2018.

Graziosi, Dean. *Millionaire Success Habits*. Dean Graziosi, 2016.

Hardy, Darren. Insane Productivity: Gain the Ultimate Success Advantage. https://dh.darrenhardy.com/insane-productivity.

Hardy, Darren. *The Compound Effect: Jumpstart Your Business, Your Life, Your Success.* New York: Vanguard Press, 2012.

Keller, Gary and Jay Papasan. *The One Thing: The Surprisingly Simple Truth Behind Extraordinary Results*. Austin, TX: Bard Press, 2013.

Maister, David. *Strategy and the Fat Smoker: Doing What's Obvious but Not Easy*. The Spangle Press, 2008.

Markovitz, Daniel. *Building the Fit Organization: Six Core Principles for Making Your Company Stronger, Faster, and More Competitive.* New York: McGraw-Hill Education, 2015.

Martin, Karen, *Clarity First: How Smart Leaders and Organizations Achieve Outstanding Performance*. New York: McGraw-Hill Education, 2018.

Martin, Karen. *The Outstanding Organization: Generate Business Results by Eliminating Chaos and Building the Foundation for Everyday Excellence*. New York: McGraw-Hill Education, 2012.

Rumelt, Richard. *Good Strategy/Bad Strategy*: *The Difference and Why It Matters*. New York: Currency, 2011.

Symchych, Phil and Alan Weiss. *The Business Wealth Builders: Accelerating Business Growth, Maximizing Profits, and Creating Wealth*. New York: Business Expert Press, 2015.

Weiss, Alan. *Thrive*. Las Brisas Research Press, 2010.

About the Author

Gary Furr is in the business of helping business owners make more money. He helps business owners and executives dramatically improve their individual and organizational effectiveness so they can take their businesses to the next level and increase their bottom line revenue.

Gary's approach has grown out of forty-plus years of C-level business experience, an MBA in organizational development, and hundreds of interactions with business owners, observing their struggles to achieve the level of success that they envisioned when they started their business.

In June of 2012 returning from an eight-day business trip to Russia, it took Gary twenty-nine hours to fly home. That is when he decided it was time to do something else, because life is short and working crazy hours is not the answer to a life well lived. Gary concluded that true wealth is not money but free time to do the things you love and be with the people you love. As CEO of Gary Furr Consulting, he is helping business owners create that same freedom for themselves.

Made in the USA
San Bernardino, CA
26 December 2018